T0275700

PCI DSS 3.1

PCI DSS 3.1
The Standard That Killed SSL

Branden R. Williams

James K. Adamson, Technical Editor

ELSEVIER

AMSTERDAM • BOSTON • HEIDELBERG • LONDON
NEW YORK • OXFORD • PARIS • SAN DIEGO
SAN FRANCISCO • SINGAPORE • SYDNEY • TOKYO

SYNGRESS,

Syngress is an imprint of Elsevier

Syngress is an imprint of Elsevier
225 Wyman Street, Waltham, MA 02451, USA

Notices
Knowledge and best practice in this field are constantly changing. As new research and
experience broaden our understanding, changes in research methods, professional practices,
or medical treatment may become necessary.

Practitioners and researchers must always rely on their own experience and knowledge in
evaluating and using any information, methods, compounds, or experiments described herein.
In using such information or methods they should be mindful of their own safety and the safety
of others, including parties for whom they have a professional responsibility.

To the fullest extent of the law, neither the Publisher nor the authors, contributors, or editors,
assume any liability for any injury and/or damage to persons or property as a matter of products
liability, negligence or otherwise, or from any use or operation of any methods, products,
instructions, or ideas contained in the material herein.

ISBN: 978-0-12-804627-2

British Library Cataloguing-in-Publication Data
A catalogue record for this book is available from the British Library

Library of Congress Cataloging-in-Publication Data
A catalog record for this book is available from the Library of Congress

For Information on all Syngress publications
visit our website at store.elsevier.com/Syngress

Working together
to grow libraries in
developing countries

www.elsevier.com • www.bookaid.org

CONTENTS

FOREWORD

"Welcome! Welcome! Kids of all ages! Step right up! The show is about to begin!"

Those words of a circus barker come to mind when thinking of someone new being introduced to the Payment Card Industry Data Security Standard (PCI DSS). Much like a spectator at the circus they're bewildered, unclear what exactly is going on or where to turn. Similar to a circus there is a great deal going on as well as a lot of noise when it comes to the PCI DSS, from the standard's governing body the PCI SSC to all of the supporting organizations, vendors, conferences, bloggers, etc.

It's been 11 years since the PCI DSS was created in 2004, and now, seven versions later, the most current version 3.1 was released in April 2015. While the standard was introduced as a compilation of best practices and policies to provide a baseline standard for the protection of cardholder data, the adaptation and evolution of the standard has been quite dynamic and has been included in state-level law in the United States including Washington in 2009[1] and Nevada in 2010.[2]

Luckily for all of us we have Dr Branden Williams and Dr Anton Chuvakin! As 'circus masters', they have come together to highlight the main 'attractions' and give insight into the standards, limitations, what scope is and can be, observations on different interpretations and implementations, and make the visits from a Payment Card Industry Qualified Security Assessor (PCI QSA) a bit less intimidating.

With over 15 years of experience in Information Security as a consultant to a C-Level executive, I have seen the challenges created by applying PCI DSS from all sides. For the past six years I have been a Managing Partner for the Enterprise Services segment of Urbane Security, a boutique consultancy of which my division specializes in complex implementations of the PCI DSS. From highly technical

---

[1]http://apps.leg.wa.gov/documents/billdocs/2009-10/Pdf/Bills/Session%20Laws/House/1149-S2.SL.pdf
[2]http://www.leg.state.nv.us/Division/Legal/LawLibrary/NRS/NRS-603A.html

and large-scale organizations to mid-sized organizations with limited resources, the challenges of meeting the intents of some of the PCI DSS controls are felt by all. Whenever I have a challenge and need to brainstorm, my first calls are to Branden or Anton as I find their thoughts align with our organization's pragmatic approach. This book is with me at all times (thank you iPad) and is a recommended reading for all of our clients who are tasked with PCI DSS compliance. This is the most approachable, accurate, and easy-to-digest guide to understanding the PCI DSS.

Erin '@SecBarbie' Jacobs

— Former CIO and CSO brings more than 15 years of consulting and c-level management experience to Urbane Security and manages the company's compliance and strategic advisory delivery teams. She and her team work with all levels of an organization to identify business goals and IT challenges and then, through specially tailored services, aligns them with the best solutions to help them securely drive their business forward. Through her work, Erin has established several industry best practices and has presented these at numerous high-profile security conferences. She is also passionate about fostering collaboration between the CSOs and practitioners who oversee day-to-day security challenges with the security research community at large to help them learn from each other and ultimately improve our industry.

ACKNOWLEDGMENTS

No matter the size of the project, publishing is never done in a vacuum. I'd like to thank my Acquisitions Editor, Chris Katsaropoulos for bringing the idea of this addendum to me. And also for dealing with my incessant requests for project updates.

I'd like to thank James Adamson, the technical editor for this book. His feedback was critical to the final product.

As always, thank you to my wife and family for encouraging me to follow my dreams and make my own dent in the universe.

And a special thanks to all of you who continue to support my efforts by buying my books, contributing to my blog, and keeping the conversation interesting when we tackle these complex and controversial topics. I'd like to think that my stance is malleable when I learn new things. A virtual high-five to you all (and a real one soon!).

Until next time!

Branden

CHAPTER 1

Introduction

If you are reading this text, you are probably just as shocked as I am that the Council released an addendum to PCI DSS outside of the normal cycle. If you think back, the last time this happened was in July of 2009 when PCI DSS v1.2.1 became public. Version 1.2.1 only had some minor changes in it that were fairly cosmetic in nature. I bet that most of you, even those who have been dealing with PCI DSS for years, probably didn't even know that there was an addendum to version 1.2.

Well, version 3.1 is no tiny update. It's nothing strictly cosmetic. It's not a tiny deal. And it's here to replace version 3.0. This addendum to PCI Compliance, 4th Edition, is meant as a companion piece. I will be taking you through the major changes in PCI DSS 3.1, including some of the fun things you will now be tasked with as you begin your assessments this fall.

For most of you, version 3.0 is still new enough that you may not have even been through your first formal 3.0 assessment. Those of you who are just now beginning to look at 3.0 should just move straight to 3.1. PCI DSS 3.0 was officially retired on June 30, 2015. If there is something in version 3.1 that may jeopardize your compliance timelines, work with your acquiring bank to figure out a pathway forward on either 3.0 or 3.1. There's really no sense in working hard to remediate gaps against a retired standard (just like you wouldn't start a PCI DSS 2.0 assessment today). Also, shame on you for waiting so long!

Those who are in the middle of your 3.0 assessment or remediation, talk to your acquiring bank. If you have already started, they may allow you to finish your validation against version 3.0. Even if this is your situation, take a look at the changes in PCI DSS 3.1. If you rely heavily on SSLv3 in your environment, this could be extremely painful. If not, the rest of the changes may be minor enough (for you) to continue forward with PCI DSS 3.1.

Now that we've discussed the themes, let's review the contents. This booklet is organized into the following chapters.

Chapter 1, Introduction. You are reading it. Good job!

Chapter 2, The Death of SSL. What exactly does it mean for you as someone who relies on SSLv3?

Chapter 3, Third Parties. An extended review of the third-party adventure that started with 3.0 and continues with 3.1.

Chapter 4, Technical Testing. More details on what technical changes exist.

Chapter 5, Other Miscellaneous Changes. For those that did not fall into the above categories, quick blurbs on what changed.

Chapter 6, Final Thoughts.

Thanks for letting me take you on this journey. What I hope you get out of this is details around the changes, business-level information that will help you choose the best path, and specific things that are actionable for you today.

CHAPTER 2

The Death of SSL

Secure Sockets Layer (SSL) is one of the foundational technologies that enabled and allowed commerce to exist in an electronic, decentralized medium. Without it (or something similar), many of us would not have the types of jobs we do today. There are a number of implementations of this historical protocol—one of the most common being the open-sourced implementation published under the OpenSSL name. We've been dealing with SSL issues in PCI DSS since version 2.0 where SSL version 2 implementations were no longer allowed due to vulnerabilities in the protocol. I can remember counseling a number of customers through the migration process. The ones that were the hardest to resolve were implementations in embedded systems or those third-party "black box" solutions that end up playing a critical role in a firm's IT environment.

Then in 2014, we had two specific vulnerabilities related to SSL that caused a bit of a ruckus through the world. The first was Heartbleed—a gruesomely named vulnerability reported by Neel Mehta from Google's Security Team. Unfortunately, this vulnerability was present in OpenSSL for a couple of years before its discovery. The vulnerability in the OpenSSL codebase was so severe and omnipresent that it forced the operators of millions of websites to revoke and reissue their SSL certificates after they patched. The bug allowed an attacker to "bleed" arbitrary amounts of data from memory revealing sensitive things like private keys that allow anyone to decrypt the SSL stream. It's like the magic decoder ring that has the power to reveal the contents of any encrypted stream. The lock in the browser was just a false sense of security.

The second was a series of vulnerabilities that started with the first POODLE attack published in October of 2014. This initial release (plus future iterations that targeted early versions of TLS) is what kicked off the process at the Council to kill SSL and early versions of Transport Layer Security (TLS) in favor of TLS 1.2 (or greater, depending on when you are reading this book). While the debate over the severity of this particular vulnerability rages, it was scored at 4.3 on the CVSS list which means you have to remediate it to remain compliant with PCI DSS.

Following this, the Council removed the three instances of SSL from PCI DSS 3.0 and the genesis for PCI DSS 3.1 was born. Given the CVSS score, it almost seems unnecessary for the Council to rush out PCI DSS 3.1 with sunset dates on SSL. Let's consider this for a moment.

PCI DSS Requirement 11.2 mandates quarterly scans of your networks. As of last October, any machine that is vulnerable to the POODLE attack is flagged as a vulnerability that needs to be fixed. Remember, any vulnerability with a CVSS score over 4.0 must be fixed in order to obtain a passing or clean scan. Therefore, if you have not solved this issue yet, then you are unable to comply with PCI DSS Requirement 11.2. So while the Council rushed to remove those words from PCI DSS 3.1, they did so (among other reasons) to make sure that these two items were in alignment. Otherwise, you would have someone trying to argue an ASV scan is wrong because the standard clearly supports the use of SSL. The reverse argument applies as well.

The tricky part, is the lack of attention on internal vulnerability scans. Companies tend to pay more attention to their external scans than internal ones because the external ones are performed by a qualified third party and may be reported directly to your bank. There tends to be more pressure to obtain clean external scans than internal ones. I'm not saying that people outright lie on their internal scans, but I sat through a number of meetings where three quarters of failing scans were explained away by the lack of a breach.

Regardless, we are here because the SSL protocol has a number of problems with it, and we now rely on TLS version 1.2 or greater for our security.

Let's also discuss some of the pressures the Council is under right now. I'm writing this from the perspective of a participant in the PCI DSS ecosystem, not someone who has any inside knowledge of what is going on at the Council. When all of this was going down, I was at a QSA/ASV company and not on the Board of Advisors. Any similarities to secret, closed-door discussions are purely coincidental.

Payment card breaches continue, with 2014 being a particularly bad year for them. The term "cyber" is gaining in popularity again and we have all kinds of government attention on information security, breaches, and the havoc they cause to our economy. It's becoming clearer that PCI DSS is not nearly as effective as it should be. There are two reasons for this. The one you will hear from the Council is that the ecosystem is not fully adhering to the Standard, thus, arguing that the Standard is not at fault for these breaches. I don't know if you can refute that argument, so let's just accept it at face value. The other reason you may hear is that the Standard is still too complex with too many shades of gray, therefore it is impossible to really comply in the first place.

> The economic drain is real. Preparing for and performing assessments isn't actually making companies any safer than they would be without these assessments. They, more accurately, tie up capital and have real opportunity cost. For more information on that, go search "the broken window fallacy" and learn how.

The real reason is somewhere in the middle. In defense of the Standard, most companies don't either take it seriously or make rational decisions about their security posture and how they process cardholder data. When we have a documented, public breach that happens with payment card data where they are found to be fully compliant with the Standard at the time of the breach, we can revisit this. More likely, we will need a string of these to really revisit how effective the Standard is at keeping cardholder data safe.

However, in defense of those trying to comply with the Standard, it needs a major overhaul. It is too complex, there is too much documentation, and every time I go about writing another version of this book I find conflicting or outdated information on the website. I could easily argue that its complex nature is the reason why it is ineffective. It's trying to be the big round hole that everyone's custom-shaped peg has to fit through. Solutions to this problem are beyond the scope of this book, but it's irresponsible for each group to point the finger at the other. Solutions come from collaboration, compromise, and cooperation. If anything, we can look to our own government and the polarizing nature politics has in our society to validate this.

Regardless of your leaning on this issue, SSL is dead and must be replaced. Companies using SSL should have been ahead of this and either not been using it at the time of the announcement, or fully upgraded shortly thereafter. Hopefully this describes you!

Migrating from SSLv3 to TLSv1.2 or later is trivial in modern systems. The Council published an overview document that may be useful for you to review.[1] It discusses many of the implications, but it doesn't go through the actual migration steps or point you to resources that could be helpful. For the most part, you only need to use a search engine to help you. Since this is quite a hot topic, most major web servers, Virtual Private Network (VPN) software providers, and other transport layer security products have well-published steps on how to do this.

Just as a quick guide for you, here are a few configuration changes you can make by product to disable SSL.

- Apache. Look for any SSL configurations and be sure to set the following: "SSLProtocol all -SSLv2 -SSLv3"
- Tomcat. Remove any sslProtocols config lines and add: "sslEnabledProtocols = "TLSv1.2""
- Java. Should be auto disabled if you keep your JDK/JRE up to date.
- IIS. Check with Microsoft on this as you will probably need to get into the registry.

Don't forget, it's not just web servers that use SSL. You may be using some version of SSL in your email, VPN, database, TN3270, and authentication servers as well. Be sure to do a thorough job of looking through your environment to find and remediate any instances of SSL v3.

As you can see, this is largely just a configuration change for most of your systems provided they are currently maintained and you have the necessary access to alter those configurations. If you have good configuration management, you may be able to push this change through fairly rapidly by changing just a few master configuration files and pushing it out to your organization. If not, this may end up being one of those nightmare scenarios that forces you to take a hard look at how you currently do configuration.

Pay particular attention to any systems that come supplied, or are fully managed, by a vendor. For current and future installations, demand a "Bill of Goods" from all of your vendors that clearly states what open-source technology is present in the device. This will help your security teams make accurate risk assessments for how new vulnerabilities truly affect your organization. As an example, the large number of stand-alone devices still vulnerable to Shellshock is, well, shocking.[2] The real kicker is that many that are still vulnerable cannot be fixed because they do not have the capacity to be upgraded.

OuchTown: population YOU, bro!

When you are going through your scanning results, make a list of every device that still responds to SSLv3 and then make your game plan. For the devices you control and can make updates to, get those changes scheduled and planned to go in your next update. Your big challenges will come with systems that are either no longer maintained—which probably put you out of compliance anyway—and outdated clients that do not support newer TLS protocols. Those of you who are still on IE 8 (or worse, IE 6) are in trouble. Any applications that use SSL will break with outdated browsers. See the note for a compatibility matrix.

> The TLS Wikipedia article has a fantastic compatibility table that may serve as a great reference for you. See that here: http://brando.ws/pcitlsmatrix

For those systems that you do not maintain, or those that you cannot access, it's time to get with the vendors to find a solution. Many of them will tell you that the versions are no longer supported and you must purchase new products. Before you unleash an expletive-laden tirade on them, ask yourself how long those systems have been in place, if they have maintenance contracts on them, and how critical they are to your business. Sometimes we blame software vendors when they cannot fix our problems, but then run systems well past their expected life. I'm looking at all the Windows XP and Windows Server 2003 users out there. In the words of a great mentor of mine, you have to participate in your own rescue. Technology is a two-way street. If you have been neglecting to pay a vendor because you didn't want to upgrade, don't get mad at them when they tell you that the only fix is to upgrade.

For these systems, you also have a rare opportunity to widen the scope of the problem to include the business. For those of you whose arm went numb when I suggested making the problem bigger, focus less on the tactical nature of removing SSL from your environment and more on using technology as a business enabler. In non-buzzword speak, go back and ask why this legacy application is in use and see if there may be a better technology alternative that will accomplish both of your goals as well as add features for the future.

Troy Leach, the current CTO of the PCI Security Standards Council, often jokes that this whole thing started when they tried to remove three words from PCI DSS 3.0. While this is a grandiose over-simplification of what is actually happening here, it's not terribly inac-curate. A quick search of SSL in PCI DSS 3.0 will find a handful of instances where it is present as part of an acceptable example to meet a requirement. The three main requirements that were updated to remove SSL as an acceptable technology are 2.2.3, 2.3, and 4.1.

REQUIREMENT 2.2.3

Requirement 2.2.3 now prohibits the use of SSL as a way to secure services, protocols, or dæmons that are inherently insecure such as NetBIOS, Telnet, FTP, and others. If you were using SSL, you simply need to look at the configuration for whatever mechanism you were leveraging to secure the transport layer and modify it to only use TLSv1.2 and greater. In cases of email, it may just be a change in the dæmon configuration. As an example, both Dovecot and Postfix (popu-lar open source email server software) allow for this configuration directly. You don't need to leverage an outside transport layer security mechanism. If you are using sTunnel to secure something like NetBIOS, you need to modify the sTunnel configuration to accomplish this.

REQUIREMENT 2.3

Next, Requirement 2.3 deals with nonconsole, administrative access. If you are in the Unix world, you are probably already using SSH so those systems are OK as is. Where you will get into trouble is if you are using any SSL VPNs to gain access into secured enclaves and then using a cleartext technology like telnet to access those systems. First off, if you are doing that, shame on you. I'm writing this in 2015, shortly after PCI DSS 3.1 became public. There is *absolutely no excuse* for using technologies like telnet or rlogin today. Jump on the SSH bandwagon and hopefully you will solve your issue. Keep in mind, if you are using SSL VPNs for any sort of segmentation, you will still need to adjust the configuration to make it comply with Requirement 4.1, which we will discuss later.

For those of you in the Windows world using RDP, make sure you have secured it appropriately. Early versions of their SSL security used TLS 1.0 which falls under the "you need to fix it" clause.

And finally, you mainframe (or large system) users. If you are using TN3270 with an SSL wrapper, you have to adjust the configuration to prohibit SSL and early versions of TLS. Depending on the version of software you are running, this may be an easy task or it could be something more painful. Many large systems also allow for SSH communication as an alternative to the SSL-wrapped TN3270. Large systems often sneak past the security department when it comes to security patches or software upgrades. I once did work for a company that only did updates to their large systems every six months (well, until PCI DSS came around anyway). If your large system is out of date (e.g., you are running a really old version of zOS), this is going to be terribly painful for you. Arguably, this falls in the category of technical debt, and it's time to pay the man.

Any other systems such as networking equipment, virtual infrastructure, or purpose-built appliances will need to be checked to see if these upgrades are required. Be sure to contact your vendor for more information and get those scheduled.

REQUIREMENT 4.1

Finally, we need to visit Requirement 4.1 to close out all of this SSL business. If you are up to date on your ASV scans, this should not be an issue at all for you. You probably had to deal with this before any holiday freeze last year, or you updated your configuration at the beginning of this year. If you haven't, your QSA is going to give you a hard time when you go to show four quarters of clean scans.

There are a number of areas where Requirement 4.1 can come into play, but for SSL it is primarily going to come in five main flavors. The first would be in any SSL VPN technology you are using to secure the connections from clients or other sites back to your offices. Not all VPNs use SSL, but it is a fairly common technology to use. If you are using an SSL VPN, you need to make the configuration change to disallow SSL and early TLS. You also may have to upgrade your software—especially on the client side—if you are not current.

Next, your websites that are in scope for PCI DSS. In the previous section, I shared a few configuration changes for Apache and IIS—two very popular web servers. This should not be an issue for most of you because it should pop up on your ASV scans. If you find web servers that have not been fixed to address this and they did not show up on your ASV scans, you might want to check to make sure they are included in your normal quarterly scan process. Chances are, they were left out.

After web servers, check any email configuration you have set up. I know it's almost ridiculous to think that this still happens, but I've added it in here for two reasons. SSL and TLS are a part of the email fabric, and many servers will automatically add this layer of protection for either passing credentials or for transmitting email content. There are still some data flows out there that may leverage email. If you are using one of those flows, be sure you check your email server configuration. The other reason why I bring it up here is that many companies will try to use single authentication sources for their employees either through LDAP or Active Directory. This means that your username and password may be the same for both your email account and some system that contains cardholder data. You need to be securing the transmission of those credentials, so make sure you make the configuration change to disallow SSL and early TLS.

For those of you who use IP-enabled payment terminals, check to make sure that you don't see either SSL or early versions of TLS as the primary protection mechanism for keeping data secure. Terminals can be a bit harder to deal with, but there are a few opportunities to resolve this. You may be able to update the configuration directly, you may take this opportunity to upgrade to a new terminal to include NFC Payments and EMV, or you may qualify for the exception listed at the end of the Requirement 4.1 notes. The note says that any terminals and their termination points "that can be verified as not being susceptible to any known exploits for SSL and early TLS may continue using these as a security control after June 30, 2016." It's a nice exemption, but I will be interested to see how QSAs and penetration testers approach this exemption. Be wary of this exemption and only use it temporarily.

Finally, any other transmissions over public networks for insecure protocols—similar to Requirement 2.2.3. Sometimes old habits die hard, and workflows may still be using protocols like FTP to batch transfer cardholder data, and those may be protected by a transport layer SSL stream. STunnel is a common tool used to accomplish this goal. This is another one that should have turned up in your ASV scans, so it shouldn't be that big of a deal.

INTERPRETATION CONFUSION

There's also an interpretation issue that I predict will pop up unless the Council specifically addresses it. With PCI DSS 3.1, we have a situation where something is permitted until the middle of 2016, while ASV scans should have been flagging these as needing to be fixed since October(ish). Which one takes precedence? Do you take your scans that are passing except for SSLv3 vulnerabilities to your QSA so he can bless you as compliant until next year? Or does your QSA point out that you have to have four quarters of *clean scans*, thus causing you to fail your validation assessment until you address the items?

If you remember, one of the goals for PCI DSS 3.0 was to remove ambiguity from the standard to make it easier for different QSAs to come to the same judgment after reviewing the facts. Interpretation variance is a significant issue with more complex environments. What should happen is that the QSA should accept any scans for existing systems only that are failing due to SSLv3 and reject any new implementations of SSLv3 that were put into production after April 15, 2015. And if you are an entity going through an assessment, don't try to fudge your dates. As a QSA, I would be highly skeptical of any system that went live in April 2015, regardless of the day. Plus, even if you pull a fast one on your QSA, you won't be able to pull a fast one on the forensic examiner that is going through your breached systems.

LONGER TIMELINES

PCI DSS 3.1 allows for some leeway if your 3.1 assessment still covers some early TLS and SSL versions that have officially sunset. Testing procedures 2.2.3.c, 2.3.f, and 4.1.i are identical representations of something called a Risk Mitigation and Migration Plan. Any existing installations must have a plan in place to reduce the risks associated with using these older versions and show how you will migrate before

June 30, 2016. Here is what your plan must contain (pulled from the aforementioned testing procedures in PCI DSS 3.1):

- Description of usage (including what data is being transmitted), types, and number of systems that use/support these prohibited technologies;
- Risk-assessment results and risk-reduction controls in place, which should use an accepted methodology performed by qualified individuals;
- Description of processes to monitor for new vulnerabilities associated with SSL/early TLS, which should be as simple as making sure your vulnerability scanners receive updates;
- Description of change control processes you alter so only accepted technology is implemented into new environments; and
- A project plan with a migration completion date no later than June 30, 2016.

Your QSA should review this plan for completeness as they must document it during your normal review.

SUMMARY OF SSL CHANGES

That's it. One acronym removed from three little requirements. *If it were only this easy.* The good news is that these requirements are not effective until June 30 of 2016—roughly four months before PCI DSS v4.0 will come out. Can you believe we're past the halfway mark in the three-year cycle?

Don't forget, there is some painful news with this update with respect to interpretation. Does a failing ASV scan trump PCI DSS 3.1, or the other way around? Ultimately, this will be up to your QSA and/ or acquiring bank. As I mentioned earlier, PCI DSS 3.1 should take precedent over a failing ASV scan for existing implementations, with one caveat. You should work to fix any externally exposed services using SSL and early TLS as soon as you can. Once those are done, work to migrate your internal systems away from SSLv3.

Joanna just received her latest vulnerability report. As expected, their legacy order management system popped up with SSL vulnerabilities. Joanna is not surprised as this system routinely shows up on vulnerability reports. Her company inherited this system through an acquisition, and some of the business users have been hanging on to this system as it was the primary system of record for the group before the acquisition. Some business processes were never converted away from this system because of a lack of an upgrade path and the cost of adding new per-seat licensing for all of the business users. Those processes are historical in nature—no new orders are placed through this system. As a security professional, Joanna knows that this system has a number of vulnerabilities, but management has never had an appetite to migrate away from the system as it was not a priority at the time.

Joanna's industry has had a number of public security breaches. While her firm has escaped thus far, management is starting to pay attention to security issues and their risks to the firm. Given the recent attention, Joanna knows that this is a great opportunity to approach management with a solution to migrating from this legacy ordering system and removing a major headache from her job responsibilities. Her plan has four phases.

Phase 1: Remove all PANs from legacy order management system. After explaining the risks to the company from this system, Joanna talks to the business users of the system to understand how they use credit card data. As it turns out, they no longer do any major research related to the PAN. The managers agree to alter their business process to use other data instead of the PAN for analysis, and Joanna is able to have Oliver, a DBA with some expertise in this legacy product, write a script to remove the PAN data from the system.

Phase 2: Move the system out of the Cardholder Data Environment (CDE). The system currently lives in the same network as the typical card processing. This makes it in scope for PCI DSS. Since no new orders are taken through this system, she works with Dan in her IT group to find a new logical home for this system in the network that is outside the CDE in another secured area of the network. As far as PCI DSS 3.1, she has removed the compliance risk after completing this task.

Phase 3: Migrate data to the currently maintained order system. Joanna works with Oliver to get the requirements for conversion as well as data replication for current business users to keep licensing costs low. She also works with procurement to ensure the firm has enough seats in their license to cover all of the business users of the product.

Phase 4: Decommission. After the data migration project, Joanna works with Dan to safely shut down the system and archive its data for archival purposes. Finally, Dan removes the server from production and safely destroys all of the data on the drive before sending the hardware off for recycling.

Phases 1 and 2 address PCI DSS 3.1, while phases 3 and 4 address the technical debt associated with neglecting this IT system. After completion, Joanna knows that her security posture and business efficiency have improved.

For these kinds of requirements, your future proofing will come in the form of staying on top of TLS technology and ensuring you are preferring the most recent version of the TLS protocol as well as being mindful of the methods you choose to enable for encryption. You will need to make sure that you maintain both the client and server ends of these connections as you make the appropriate configuration changes.

As you procure technology for use in your environment, be sure you are aware of the expected lifespan of that particular piece of equipment. Do they expect you to upgrade or replace it within three to four years? Be sure you include that in your modeling. In addition, ask for a Bill of Goods with your purchase so that you know any third-party code—especially open source—that is included as part of the products' inner workings. You need to make sure that the vendor has a method to upgrade any vulnerable code inside these systems for the next Heartbleed or Shellshock vulnerability.

Of course, for the "over the wire" data protection component, you could always change to a different type of transport layer encryption. Both IPSec and SSH make for decent alternatives to SSL or TLS—but there is no guarantee that either is free from security vulnerabilities. In addition, any open source tools that may be deployed to enable these transports must be maintained as above (think OpenSSH or Openswan as examples). As with most security problems, stay on top of your systems and make sure you update them in a timely manner.

NOTES

1. See http://brando.ws/pcissltls.
2. For more information on Shellshock, visit http://shellshocker.net.

Third Parties

Third parties have always been a challenge for PCI DSS. In fact, a tidbit from some Visa CISP lore suggests that this whole PCI DSS mess stemmed from the lack of Visa's visibility into the third parties that may be handling data on behalf of merchants. PCI DSS 3.0, and now 3.1, is focusing more closely on those third parties, but third parties have always been an issue for PCI DSS. There have always been requirements for managing relationships with third parties through contracts and risk assessments, and the last few versions of the standard have gradually stepped up these requirements. I would be wary of a QSA who didn't ask to see lots of documentation from your third parties. In some instances, he should suggest (and perform) a site visit. In the next section, we will cover the clarification as well as review all the third-party requirements.

Keen PCI DSS gurus might be wondering why I'm even calling this out as a separate section. No, I am not paid by the word (wouldn't that be nice!), but I still see a lot of confusion around third parties and how to handle them. The clarification for third parties in PCI DSS 3.1 is pretty minor, and almost looks more like a formatting change than a requirement change. The Summary of Changes document simply suggests a clarification of how a third party can demonstrate compliance. On the surface, I'm not sure what party was complaining about this, but it is fairly clear now. Third parties must either have their own yearly assessment performed, which probably should lead to registration with a sponsor bank and being listed on a compliant service provider list, or they can respond to assessment requests on behalf of their customers. These were present in PCI DSS 3.0, however, they are more explicitly stated in 3.1 with terms like "Annual Assessment," and "Multiple, On-Demand Assessments."

If you are a third party who is reading this book wondering why your customers are constantly coming to you with assessment requests, please read page 12 of PCI DSS 3.1. I would also strongly suggest you choose the first path so that you can go through the process one time per year instead of many, many, many times as you respond to these on-demand requests. I would also strongly suggest going through the process to get listed as a compliant service provider. After going through an assessment, the process to get registered and listed is not too difficult and is mostly a paperwork exercise. Getting on these lists varies by payment brand, but your QSA should know how to help you here. If not, work with your customer (who is probably a merchant) to get listed through their acquiring institution.

REQUIREMENT 12.9

This is not a new requirement, but as we mentioned in the last book, there are some new teeth to it as of PCI DSS 3.0. After June 30, 2015, service providers must demonstrate that their contracts are updated to include PCI DSS compliance responsibility and language. Most of them should have this as Requirement 12.8.2's PCI DSS 3.0 clarification requires that the language exists in some document that supports the business relationship between the two firms.

If you are still struggling with this because of a stubborn service provider, it's time to start looking for alternatives. Today, there are tons of firms that would love to compete for your business and happily include that language. I realize there are other constraints such as price, technology integrations, and business relationships that may be problematic, but this is a protection that you need for PCI DSS compliance and should want for your own risk-management peace of mind.

CALL THE BALL

I was recently on a panel with some PCI DSS experts and an audience member asked how she was supposed to comply with PCI DSS with shrinking budgets and headcount constraints. I know how serious of a problem this can be for institutions. PCI DSS and compliance simply are not areas where the business wants to invest. Paraphrasing our back and forth in front of the audience, I asked her if she ultimately has control over how she processes cardholder data. Meaning, could she change her processing agreement to get a more favorable outcome? She said she did, and I responded with something like, "You should look for a processor that you can outsource all of your responsibility or PCI DSS to." It might be a P2PE solution or an encrypting, leased terminal. Will she be paying more per transaction? Probably, but her organization will be able to attach the cost of processing, which should include securing the transaction and complying with PCI DSS, more closely to the action of processing a card.

Wherever you are out there, I hope you found a great new vendor that could solve your problem!

CHAPTER 4

Technical Testing

Technical testing has a long-standing legacy in PCI DSS. Even from the days of the old CISP and SDP standards, technical testing has been a critical component of demonstrating compliance. Over the years, testing has evolved from simple external scans to full penetration testing that requires testers to prod all layers of the OSI model. In PCI DSS 3.0, the Standard requires that you use an industry-accepted penetration-testing methodology, which could lead to confusion. They do cite NIST SP 800-115 as an example methodology and the Penetration Testing Guidance (March 2015) by the Council, which at least gives you a place to start. Penetration testing is not something that you should take lightly, and not something you should treat as a slightly more difficult vulnerability scan. True penetration testing almost always leads to a successful intrusion, and should target people and process as diligently as it targets technology.

PCI DSS 3.1 provided some fairly critical updates to version 3.0 that help to clarify the intent of the new penetration-testing requirements. Specifically, they wanted to clarify how segmentation would be tested, what needs to be included for the testing, and how to ensure blocking and alerting technology works to the best of its ability.

Since technical testing is in a couple of different requirements, we're going to be jumping around a bit. This section primarily focuses on updates to Requirement 11.3 and 6.6.

REQUIREMENT 11.3

This requirement evolved in two ways. First, the Council removed some language from the 11.3.2.a testing procedure. Next, they updated Requirement 11.3.4 to help clarify what systems must be tested for segmentation. Remember, as of PCI DSS 3.0, any declared "segmentation" in your environment must be validated as part of this process.

As you are going through your preparation for your annual assessment, consider reviewing the 11.3 language very carefully. Your QSA is going to be asking a few more questions this time around, specifically around your methodology and ensuring the report from your test aligns with that methodology. You will need to take networks and applications through this process, and you will probably have many more findings this year. In addition, while you are required to make sure that you test for any vulnerability listed in Requirement 6.5, be sure your methodology includes a run through the latest OWASP Top 10 as well.

REQUIREMENT 6.6

This requirement seems to get more teeth with every iteration. When it was first introduced, it was effectively neutered by Requirement 11.3. Or Requirement 6.6 neutered Requirement 11.3. It's all a matter of perspective. Essentially, companies could choose to (effectively) follow the penetration testing requirements from 11.3 for their web applications, or they could superfluously add a Web Application Firewall (WAF). WAFs have a place in your information security strategy, but it should not be hastily slapped in place based on Requirement 6.6. The current iteration in 3.1 is still a bit confusing. Here's how you need to look at it. You must do one of these two things.

1. You must take any public facing application through Requirement 11.3, or
2. You must deploy a WAF in front of said public facing web application.

Am I oversimplifying things? Slightly. But the review of both requirements would be nearly identical (albeit with more specific guidance in 6.6).

If you choose to deploy a WAF, PCI DSS 3.1 closes another loophole with deployments that alert instead of block. The new update now requires that alerts are "immediately investigated." The guidance uses weaker language and says that the response must be "timely." You can guess that there will be interpretation variance on this. Here's my guidance. If you are using a WAF, then you should tune it to be tied to an alerting system that is immediately followed up on. Or, better yet, set it to actively start blocking bad traffic. If you do either of these things poorly, I can assure you that it will be held over your head in the case of a breach.

You should probably use a combination. I would argue the better strategy is to take it through Requirement 11.3 and ensure you fully meet that requirement. Then, for added measure, drop the WAF in place in alert mode, and develop a risk-based strategy for responding to the alerts. Ultimately, this meets the requirement without the WAF, but putting additional detection technologies in place may help you detect more attacks before they get serious. Check with your security teams to see what kind of technologies they recommend!

Future proofing against technical testing is painful, but it's absolutely possible. Essentially, it means that you are altering your testing methodology and techniques to keep up with current hacking trends—including specific attacks against the technology in use at your firm. For example, if you decide to take on a mobile payments offering, you need to adjust your methodology to include the apps, devices, and infrastructure you stand up that is dedicated to this function. Keeping up with general application vulnerabilities as well as vulnerabilities rooted in your platform is a must, and being able to react to those changes as they pop up is critical. If you have not embraced faster moving IT deployment methods such as DevOps, it's probably time to consider moving in that direction. Keep in mind, PCI DSS doesn't keep up with the bad guys, so if you want to stay safe, you need to.

CHAPTER 5

Other Miscellaneous Changes

There are a number of requirements that had minor updates in PCI DSS 3.1, but didn't really group together as one of the major issues identified earlier. As you review the Summary of Changes from PCI DSS 3.0 to 3.1 document, spend some time looking through the first ten items on page 3. Those are items that are either general changes, changes specific to the various front-matter sections, or as the first item says, fixing a typo. I found a couple while writing the last book and sent them over to the team. It could be things like missing bullets, formatting, or other minor changes that don't alter the meaning or interpretation of the standard itself. For the other nine mentioned, these are specific clarifications that are clearly pointed out for you to consider.

REQUIREMENT 3.2.1–3.2.3

Storage and usage of sensitive authentication data is massively debated when it comes to scoping and performing PCI DSS assessments. The update in 3.1 puts to bed a long-standing quandary of where this requirement comes into play. There seems to have been a gap in the handoff between the first QSAs and the current user base. The requirement now states that the storage of sensitive authentication data (SAD) is not permitted "after authorization." If your ability to process is temporarily suspended, you are permitted to perform a Store and Forward for any authorizations that are unable to process due to an outage.

Some advice for this requirement... Your goal, as a target for hackers, should be to remove any SAD immediately after it is used and ensure any payment applications comply with PA-DSS. If you need to do a pre-authorization and then full authorization once you have the total amount, pre-authorize with all the SAD, and then do a full authorization without the SAD. After usage, securely scrub the stored data to ensure

that it is completely removed from these systems. This is the same guidance in the big book as well as the same guidance you will find on many
industry blogs (including mine).

The next step you should consider is doing some level of encryption
so that a compromised POS controller would not impact the security
of this data. There are a number of options available to you today.
Those include acquirer-provided solutions, such as TransArmor from
First Data, or P2PE-validated solutions, such as Bluefin's PayConex.
Whatever solution you choose, there are a few elements that you
should consider in your solution:

1. Does the solution use industry-accepted encryption algorithms?
2. Does the solution return tokens to you so you are no longer handling
   PAN data after the auth?
3. Will you be EMV-enabled after the solution?
4. Will you be able to accept Apple Pay and Samsung Pay after the
   solution?

At a minimum, you should ensure the first three items on the list are
checked off. Given the impending liability shift related to EMV deployments coming up in October of 2015, you want to be on the "enabled"
side of that equation—especially since one of the larger retail banks
(Chase) has finally started issuing chip cards. Many banks have multiple
options for different security features.[1] Apple Pay and Samsung Pay
may not be needed or desired for your particular solution, but there are
advantages to putting either or both in your environment. Keep in
mind, there are still many other payment methods that we have not discussed that are outside the scope of PCI DSS. For those, you should
work with your acquirer or processor to add those mechanisms to your
particular processing options.

TESTING PROCEDURE 3.4.E

Keen observers now see a new testing procedure for Requirement 3.4
based on the note added in PCI DSS 2.0 about the issues with hashing
and truncation. The new testing procedure requires QSA to "examine
implemented controls to verify that the hashed and truncated versions
cannot be correlated to reconstruct the original PAN." Even though
this note has been present as far back as PCI DSS 2.0, this is the first

time we see a testing procedure to validate that an assessed entity is not doing this behavior. This testing procedure may trip you up as you go through your first 3.1 assessment in areas where you have ignored the note in the requirement.

Bad guys can create rainbow tables, or precomputed tables that contain a PAN and hashed value, in very little time with readily available technology. If you use a hash, but then also store a truncated version of the PAN (as an example, first six, last four), there are only so many variations of those middle six digits that will yield a valid PAN. Once you calculate those, building a hash table is just one added step. Now an attacker has essentially reversed your one-way hashing algorithm and has all the original PAN data.

Hashing, in general, is something that has fallen in and out of favor as a protection mechanism for cards. The reason why it was so attractive at first is because it is a one-way hash. In fact, I even wrote articles about it in the mid-2000s proclaiming it as a great solution for protecting card data. I still think it has great uses, but there is a catch in how we treat hashed data that is unique to these algorithms. Hashes are one-way algorithms—meaning, there is no mathematical way to go from a hash to the original value. This is unlike crypto routines where Alice takes plaintext, encrypts it using a key, and sends it to Bob to decrypt with his key. In this case, the message is hidden from the transport medium.

If we take the same analogy and apply it to hashing, Alice takes her plaintext and runs it through a hashing mechanism—potentially with a key, referred to as a salt—and sends it to Bob. Alice has effectively hidden the message from the transport medium as well as the recipient. Bob cannot convert that hash back into a plaintext value to read. To use an old phrase, you can turn oranges into orange juice, but you can't turn orange juice back into oranges.

It's for this reason that we run into problems. Encrypted data is protected by a key, but you don't see companies leaving their encrypted data lying around in plain sight for anyone to take. Hashed data is another form of encrypted data, but because it cannot be mathematically reversed, many firms have been relaxed with the protection of this hashed data.

Now let's say that Alice will only send Bob one of 1000 messages. Alice may want to signal Bob using one of those predetermined messages as a trigger that an event is going to happen. If Bob knows all of those messages and knows the key or salt, Bob can precompute all the possible hashes from the 1000 predetermined messages and match one to the hash from Alice. The transport medium cannot read the message, but Bob will ultimately know what Alice sent. Aside from the obviously nefarious uses for this, PANs can suffer the same fate. The difference between PAN data and the Alice and Bob messages is that we already know and can precompute every possible PAN—regardless if it is tied to an open account. So if a bad guy compromises some hashed data that includes truncated data, you shortcut the work he has to do to obtain an original PAN.

If you leverage hashing in your environment, it's time to ensure you are not coupling that with any kind of truncation that could trip you up on this testing procedure.

REQUIREMENT 4.2

This clarification is unfortunately necessary, but anyone who argued that SMS didn't apply to this requirement was really kidding themselves. I could see an argument for SMS as part of that old carrier-grade exemption, but I don't know how you would work around the GSM and CDMA notes in Requirement 4.1. If it smells like end-user messaging technologies, treat it like that. Think of all the other versions of end-user messaging that are not listed in the examples, such as Kik, Cyber Dust, Wickr, Snapchat (hah), What'sApp, Facebook Messenger, Slack, and even Twitter DMs. Keep your PANs away from anything like that.

REQUIREMENT 8.1.4 AND 8.2.4

Let's tackle these two requirements together as the change is interrelated. In the 4th edition of PCI Compliance, we discussed how the ambiguity in PCI DSS is getting a bit out of whack. Words like "should" and "periodic" increased dramatically from PCI DSS 2.0 to 3.0. Another ambiguous term could be "at least," I suppose. PCI DSS clarified Requirement 8.1.4 to remove the word "at least" in favor of the word "within," and Requirement 8.2.4 to add the word "once" after the phrase "at least." My only advice to those of you out there who feel wronged by this change is to stop trying to out-smart the requirements. Your efforts would be better off spent trying to reduce your scope through end-to-end encryption or outsourcing than it will through bickering about a few words that might get you an extra few weeks out of a password change.

REQUIREMENT 9.2

This one is such a minor change that I feel like this was clearly an issue identified within a few weeks of the original 3.0 publication. There are two chances to this requirement. The first comes in the 9.2.a testing procedure where the word "new" was removed from the first (actual) bullet. There is a formatting mistake corrected right above it, so we'll assume that the first bullet in 3.1 is what was intended as the first bullet for 3.0. I can see how the word "new" would trip folks up who are reading in to the words literally, but the requirement is identical between 3.0 and 3.1. Just the testing procedures changed. In addition, the Council combined testing procedures 9.2.b and 9.2.d to account for a redundancy issue.

TESTING PROCEDURE 9.9.1.B

This is another minor wording change to more clearly state what is being asked in the testing procedure. The intent of the testing procedure was to ensure a QSA was looking at both the location of the device as well as the device itself when considering the accuracy of the list. Fairly simple clarification, but we're going to spend a few paragraphs here talking about the challenges with Requirement 9.9 and what you need to be doing to address them.

Requirement 9.9 is designed to add a layer of protection on one of the most visible parts of the cardholder data environment—the payment terminal. Over the last several years, these devices have been under increasing scrutiny by both attackers and the payment card industry at large. Terminals are subject to standards that have evolved specifically to add controls to the terminal itself through physical and electronic hardening. Since these devices are the first interaction with a payment card, the right kind of compromise could yield criminals with thousand PANs.

Terminals can be vulnerable to tampering. A determined attacker with access to dummy terminals may find a weakness that allows them to place skimming devices into the terminal itself. Examples where this has happened in the past include attackers drilling small holes into terminals to expose parts of the electronics and tiny skimmers placed inside or around the terminal housing. In order to combat some of the more blatant attempts to tamper with terminals, the PCI Security Standards Council added a new requirement to version 3.0 of PCI DSS—now in effect as of July, 2015.

PCI DSS gives merchants the flexibility to use a number of different methods to comply with any of its requirements. At any given time, you should have full records that include the make and model of the device, its specific location, the serial number of the device, and specific details on how this terminal has been inspected for possible tampering or substitution with a record of all of those inspections and findings. Additional items you may want to record include its projected lifespan, contacts for support, replacement costs, and potential upgrade paths. All of those items together, provided they are consistently kept up to date with a relatively short period of inspection time (such as weekly) demonstrates to an auditor or assessor that you are fully meeting this requirement.

For a small merchant, the case for a manual or automated compliance tool comes down to the manager or owner's ability to handle a mandated routine process. Evidence of missed inspection points or missing records will definitely point to a noncompliance issue—especially in the aftermath of a breach. For a small merchant, this may be enough to determine cause in the breach, which would eventually lead to fines. For managers or owners who have either multiple locations and/or larger footprints with multiple terminals (including multiple terminal brands), compliance most likely requires some level of automation or a technology tool. It is possible to do manually, but it's impractical with the intensity of manual work required to fully comply with these requirements. Given that manual, repetitive work may lead to apathy in the individuals performing the tasks, large merchants should consider using a tool to help detect any type of tampering or alterations of the device. In addition, many individuals may not be qualified to properly look for tampering in terminals if they have not had recent briefings on current attack trends.

Modern payment terminals come with countermeasures to help detect tampering and can even disable themselves or send alert codes to anyone listening that there is a problem. Criminals are creative—physical inspection is still paramount to detecting skimmers.

Given our challenges with skimming, is Requirement 9.9 enough to keep you safe? Let us not forget that changes to PCI DSS are reactive and slow. The bad guys know exactly what is required to meet the standard, and thanks to the slow adoption of PCI DSS changes, they have plenty of lead time to figure out how to get around the requirements in PCI DSS. Even the Council will tell you that compliance with PCI DSS is not enough to prevent a breach and should not be the high water mark by which you build your security and compliance program. Thus, while compliance with PCI DSS is required, it should be done so as a by-product of a solid information security program.

If your business is in an area prone to attacks on terminals, or it is one that uses unattended payment terminals such as automated fuel dispensers, Requirement 9.9 is not enough to keep those points of interaction safe. For additional protection, consider the following where it is reasonably possible to do with minimal business impact:

- Ensure that any locks on unattended payment terminals are changed and not commonly keyed.
- Understand the inner workings of each technology and follow their implementation guides to the letter.
- Routinely inspect the devices for tampering (for instance, at every shift change).
- Place cameras around these devices so that you can capture individuals tampering with them, but not in a way that would capture a customer's PIN.
- Ensure you receive vendor updates to include security patches and alerts to exploits that defeat antitampering controls.
- Reward employees for spotting and alerting management to suspicious behavior.
- Set reasonable technology lifespans for terminals and replace at their end of life.
- Be a maniacal record keeper.
- Fully understand the controls surrounding your terminals, where you need to augment them, and exactly what liabilities may sit at your feet in the case of a breach (as a hint, you won't be able to blame that third-party reseller or integrator).

Hopefully this extended review of the effects of Requirement 9.9 helps to illustrate the significant amount of work required to meet this requirement.

REQUIREMENT 10.6.1

The changes to this requirement are pretty minor. If you put versions 3.0 and 3.1 side by side, you will see a few edits, but nothing really substantial. The official wording is that the requirement was altered to "more clearly differentiate intent from Requirement 10.6.2." Just keep in mind that you need to actually review your security logs, pay attention to the alerts that your systems are generating, and allocate proper resources to manage all the events that your information security systems will generate.

REQUIREMENT 11.5

The Council struggles with the demands from the community when it comes to defining terms. At times, the Council does not want to add examples because it may cause a revision in the standard (e.g., the SSL issue we've been over) or because it may cause a QSA to become hyper focused on *only* those examples. In the case of Requirement 11.5, the Council added some examples of what "unauthorized modification(s)" might include. The examples they added are "changes, additions, and deletions." Or, in reality, all the things that any proper file integrity monitoring solution will check for and alert.

REQUIREMENT 12.2

As a QSA, one of my favorite things to do was to review a merchant's risk assessment process and final report. I enjoyed it because you could quickly determine how painful the assessment process was going to be based on how well they handled their internal risk analysis. For the most part, merchants were well intentioned in their risk assessments. What they lacked was consistency, methodologies for determining risk in a repeatable manner, accurate scope, and recency. The requirement says at least annually and after significant changes to the environment. What constitutes a significant change is always up for debate, but risk assessments were usually not performed often enough.

For every decent attempt at a risk assessment, there were people going through the motions for the sole purpose of trying to meet a compliance requirement. Good QSAs caught this and would question the validity of the assessment. Poor ones just looked at the cover page and checked the box. I often wonder if merchants put as much effort into risk assessments as they do trying to get out of meeting PCI requirements; breaches would be dramatically lower.

For PCI DSS 3.1, you now must ensure your risk assessment results in a "formal, documented analysis of risk." I imagine that there are managers shuddering after reading that. Once it's on paper, your firm may be obligated to something about the risk—including disclosing it. If you are doing good risk assessments today, not much should change for you. If you've been avoiding formal documentation, it's time to get with your legal and audit teams to figure out what you need to do and how you need to do it. Don't expect them to define the methodology for you, but they may have certain things in place that you can leverage.

SUMMARY

This section included a hodgepodge of other changes in the standard that didn't really fit into the other chapters we called out, and really couldn't stand on their own as a chapter. Remember, you need to review your latest assessment report and go side-by-side with the new requirements to see what might need to change. Be sure to note those items and add them as new findings. Then, work to close them so when you do your first 3.1 validation it goes as smoothly as possible.

NOTE

1. See a list here: http://brando.ws/emvlist2015.

CHAPTER 6

Final Thoughts

As you wade through the changes document for PCI DSS 3.1, you may notice that there were a few items mentioned there that are not mentioned in this text. For the sake of brevity, any requirements that had minor clarifications of intent were not included in the text (outside of the Third-Party issue because it needs reinforcing). The owner of the Standard is the PCI Security Standards Council, and all of the official documentation can be downloaded from their website at http://www.pcisecuritystandards.org/. For enforcement issues, check with your acquirer to work through the payment brands. For any interpretation issues, check with your QSA. The Council is not an enforcement arm, they don't want to see your ROC, and they really don't provide meaningful guidance.

An example of such a change would be the alteration to the compensating control worksheet completed example. Unix admins and QSAs have surmised that the Council actually meant to include the use of "sudo" not "su" when describing how multiple admins can "share" a root account. You can imagine that a 112-page document is going to have oversights like this—some of which may even exist as long as this one. This is where the feedback process becomes critical for all to participate in, to ensure the Standard is in alignment with the risks we face every day.

PCI DSS 3.1 still leaves many of the same unanswered questions we had in PCI DSS 3.0. There still is no linkage to emerging technology when it comes to the Standard itself—which is especially frustrating when you count the sheer volume of pages the Council produces as guidance. There is no mention of cloud, even though nearly every business is leveraging it in some form or fashion. And mobile is still sort of sticking out there without clear guidance.

Regardless of the editorial, the changes in PCI DSS 3.1 are overall positive on a plus–minus scale. We are officially out of the feedback period for PCI DSS 3.0, but that doesn't mean you can't send the Council your comments. They do read the feedback, so be sure to submit something that is based on fact and is well presented. The more you can provide and give to the Council, the better.

I hope you have enjoyed this review of the changes introduced in PCI DSS 3.1. As always, you can find me at my website at http://www.brandenwilliams.com/ with all of my publications. I'm also typically at the major information security shows and have recently been doing quite a few shows in the payments space. If you have any suggestions for future revisions of this book, drop me a line!

Until next time!

Printed in the United States
By Bookmasters